discovermore

Forms of Energy

What Is Mechanical Energy?

Virginia Elliott

Britannica Educational Publishing

IN ASSOCIATION WITH

THE ROSEN PUBLISHING GROUP

Published in 2026 by Britannica Educational Publishing (a trademark of Encyclopædia Britannica, Inc.) in association with The Rosen Publishing Group, Inc.
2544 Clinton Street, Buffalo, NY 14224

Distributed exclusively by Rosen Publishing.
To see additional Britannica Educational Publishing titles, go to rosenpublishing.com.

Editor: Danielle Haynes
Book Design: Michael Flynn

Photo Credits: Cover New Africa/Shutterstock.com; (series background) Dai Yim/Shutterstock.com; p. 4 PeopleImages.com - Yuri A/Shutterstock.com; p. 5 IM Imagery/Shutterstock.com; p. 6 CLOUD-WALKER/Shutterstock.com; p. 7 Antonio Guillem/Shutterstock.com; p. 8 Brandon Woyshnis/Shutterstock.com; p. 9 Master1305/Shutterstock.com; p. 10 Alexapicso/Shutterstock.com; p. 11 rawf8/Shutterstock.com; p. 13 (top) voronaman/Shutterstock.com; p. 13 (bottom) mlopez/Shutterstock.com; p. 15 (all) Liderina/Shutterstock.com; p. 16 K-FK/Shutterstock.com; p. 17 BlueRingMedia/Shutterstock.com; p. 18 CGN089/Shutterstock.com; p. 19 Koldunov/Shutterstock.com; p. 20 mar_tin/Shutterstock.com; p. 21 Nikolay 007/Shutterstock.com; p. 22 hrui/Shutterstock.com; p. 23 Evgeny_V/Shutterstock.com; p. 24 kheartmanee thongyot/Shutterstock.com; p. 25 lala firdaa/Shutterstock.com; p. 27 (top) testing/Shutterstock.com; p. 27 (bottom) brgfx/Shutterstock.com; p. 28 Christie Cooper/Shutterstock.com; p. 29 Ryan DeBerardinis/Shutterstock.com.

Cataloging-in-Publication Data

Names: Elliott, Virginia (Children's writer).
Title: Mechanical energy / Virginia Elliott.
Description: New York : Britannica Educational Publishing, in association with Rosen Educational Services, 2026. | Series: Discover more: forms of energy | Includes glossary and index.
Identifiers: ISBN 9781641905725 (library bound) | ISBN 9781641905718 (pbk) | ISBN 9781641905732 (ebook)
Subjects: LCSH: Force and energy--Juvenile literature. | Power (Mechanics)--Juvenile literature. | Motion--Juvenile literature.
Classification: LCC QC73.4 E455 2026 | DDC 531.6--dc23

Manufactured in China

CPSIA Compliance Information: Batch #QWBRIT26. For further information contact Rosen Publishing at 1-800-237-9932.

Contents

Energy Basics 4
Kinetic and Potential Energy 6
What Is Mechanical Energy? 8
Mass and Position 10
Transforming Energy 12
Where Is Mechanical Energy? 14
Putting in the Work 16
Using Energy Every Day 18
Mechanical Energy Through History 20
Sustainable Energy 22
Fossil Fuels 24
Problems with Fossil Fuels 26
Changing Energy Use 28
Glossary 30
For More Information 31
Index 32

Energy Basics

Energy is the ability to do work. It's another word for power. Energy makes things move. It makes machines work. Energy also makes living things grow. The sun is the source of almost all energy on Earth. The sun makes plants grow. When humans and animals eat the plants, they gain energy from the chemical energy that is stored in the plants. Humans get energy to move and run from eating food.

The sun gives energy to plants, people, and animals.

Machines such as robot arms in factories, cars, and even bicycles use mechanical energy to move.

Energy exists in many different forms. Electrical energy is used to power televisions and computers. This energy is created when particles called electrons move from one **atom** to another. Heat and light are also forms of energy. A dog's bark is an example of sound energy. The energy that an object or a body holds because of its motion and its position is called mechanical energy. Humans use mechanical energy to move, do work, and play.

WORD WISE

AN ATOM IS A TINY PARTICLE. ATOMS ARE THE BUILDING BLOCKS OF ALL MATTER.

Kinetic and Potential Energy

When we think of energy, we think of movement, also known as kinetic energy. But some things that don't seem to move have what's called potential energy. Potential energy is stored energy. For example, the chemical energy of food is stored energy. When people eat, their bodies change the stored energy into moving energy.

When an archer pulls and holds the string on their bow, it's potential energy. When they release the string and arrow, the arrow has kinetic energy.

The energy used to walk is kinetic energy, while the energy stored in the food you eat is potential energy.

Potential energy can also come from the position of an object. For example, a rock on top of a hill has potential energy because it could roll down the hill.

Kinetic energy is moving energy. Once the rock starts rolling down the hill it gains kinetic energy and loses potential energy. Electrical energy is kinetic energy because it consists of tiny particles called electrons that move from one atom to another. These electrons orbit around the center of an atom in layers called electron shells.

Consider This

A player lifts a bowling ball, takes aim, and rolls it down the alley. The ball strikes all 10 pins! Is this an example of potential or kinetic energy—or both?

What Is Mechanical Energy?

Mechanical energy is a unique form of energy. It can exist as both potential energy and kinetic energy. An object or a body possesses mechanical energy because of its motion (kinetic energy) and its position (potential energy).

Cars have potential energy in their fuel and kinetic energy when the parts move.

The muscles in your legs—and elsewhere in your body—have both potential and kinetic energy.

An object can do work if it has mechanical energy. Machines use mechanical energy to perform work, such as cars driving on roads. Animals use mechanical energy to do work as well, such as when birds fly through the air or fish swim in the sea.

Humans also use mechanical energy to do work. For instance, a person uses mechanical energy to score a goal in a soccer game. When the person's foot extends back, it has potential energy. When the foot kicks forward, the potential energy turns into kinetic energy to drive the ball into the goal. Humans get that mechanical energy from the chemical energy stored in food.

Consider This

People use mechanical energy to swing back and forth on playground swings. At what point will the swing have the most potential energy?

Mass and Position

Matter is anything that takes up space and has mass. Air, water, rocks, and even people are examples of matter. Matter can be described by its mass. The mass of an object is the amount of material that makes up the object. The greater the mass of an object, the greater potential energy it can have. For instance, a bowling ball has more mass than a beach ball. The bowling ball at rest on a hill has more potential energy than the beach ball at rest on a hill.

An object's height or position is another factor that determines its amount of potential energy. An object at a great height or position will have greater energy than the same object at a lower height.

A beach ball may be bigger than a bowling ball, but it's filled with air, so it has less mass.

Consider This

How can you tell that a bowling ball has more mass than a beach ball? What is inside each of them?

Transforming Energy

One of the most important laws in science is that energy cannot be created or destroyed. It can neither appear out of nowhere nor vanish into nowhere. One form of energy can be converted into another, though. Sometimes this happens naturally. For example, a person opening a door uses chemical energy stored in muscles. This energy is converted to mechanical energy of the moving muscle.

People have also learned how to use one form of energy to produce another. A battery is a device that stores power until it is needed. The stored power is in the form of chemical energy. That changes into electrical energy when the battery is used. In a light bulb, electrical energy changes to light and heat energy. A car's engine converts the chemical energy in fuel or batteries into moving mechanical energy.

compareandcontrast

How is the chemical energy that comes from food like the chemical energy that comes from car fuel? How is it different?

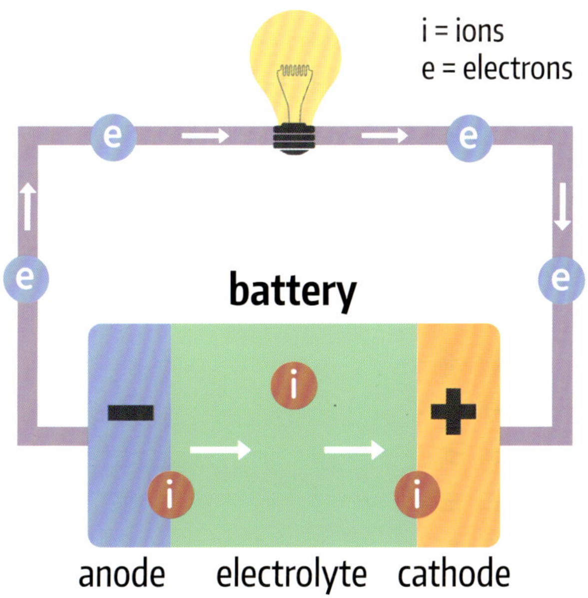

Chemical energy inside a battery is found in a paste called an electrolyte. When you connect the ends of the battery to a device such as a lightbulb, the electrons in the electrolyte travel to turn on the light.

Where Is Mechanical Energy?

Mechanical energy is all around us all the time, even on the playground. Swinging on a swing set is an example of mechanical energy. Another example is playing on a slide. At the top of the slide, the body has the greatest potential energy and great height or position. The body has zero kinetic energy at this point because it is not moving. As the person slides down, the potential energy changes to kinetic energy. The total potential energy plus kinetic energy still equals the same amount of mechanical energy. In this case, the force of **gravity** helps provide the kinetic energy.

When going down a slide, some of the energy transforms to heat energy due to friction. Have you ever noticed that your legs might feel a little warm as they rub against the slide surface?

Even when sitting still at the top of a slide, the human body has mechanical energy. The heart moves as it pumps blood through the body, your eyelids move as you blink, and your lungs expand to bring in air.

WORD WISE

GRAVITY IS A FORCE OF ATTRACTION BETWEEN OBJECTS THAT PULLS OBJECTS TOGETHER. THE MORE MASS AN OBJECT HAS, THE STRONGER ITS FORCE OF GRAVITY IS. THE PLANET EARTH HAS MORE MASS THAN ANYTHING ON IT SO IT PULLS ALL THINGS TOWARD IT.

Putting in the Work

All forms of energy do work, but mechanical energy is especially good at this. Machines—from simple tools such as wedges, levers, and pulleys to complex devices such as automobiles—use mechanical energy to do work. A demolition machine is a good example. The machine's huge wrecking ball has great mass. As the ball swings backward, its high position holds great potential energy. When the ball swings forward and hits a structure, the force or work of mechanical energy brings down the structure.

A wrecking ball exhibits mechanical energy as it swings back and forth, but it gets energy from the chemical energy in the fuel in the machine.

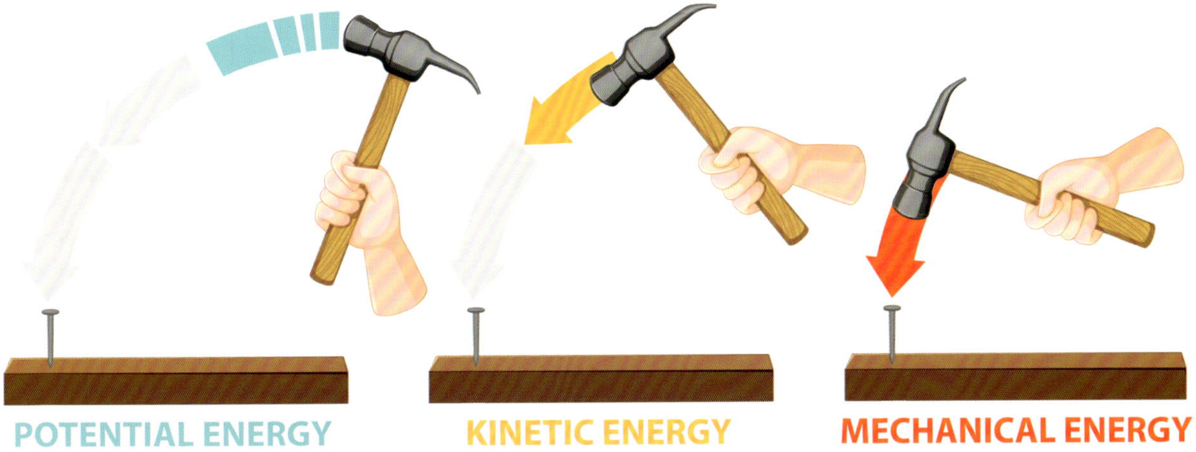

The hammer has potential, kinetic, and mechanical energy, but so does your arm, which is helping fuel the work.

Humans also use the mechanical energy of simple tools to do work. For instance, a hammer has mechanical energy when it is used to drive a nail into a board. When the hammer is raised, it has potential energy from the work done in lifting it. When the hammer is moved toward the nail, the potential energy becomes kinetic energy, which can do the work of driving the nail into the board. When you set the hammer down on the table, it has potential energy to fall to the floor (though not likely if the table is flat and sturdy).

Consider This

There are many examples of mechanical energy in nature, too. What work gets done from the mechanical energy of a river?

Using Energy Every Day

Humans use mechanical energy every day. All actions done by the body, such as lifting a fork to the mouth, require mechanical energy. Human bodies convert the chemical energy found in food into energy to fuel movements. Even when the body is at rest, the human heart constantly transforms the body's stored fuel into the mechanical energy of blood pumping throughout the body.

Put your hand over your heart. Can you feel the mechanical energy as your heart beats and pumps blood?

This gas stove uses the chemical energy from gas to create heat energy to cook foods. The chef used the mechanical energy in his hands to turn on the stove.

Sometimes our actions themselves lead to other uses of mechanical energy. Flipping on a fan's switch converts the electrical energy into mechanical energy that makes the fan's blades turn and move. Turning on the stove converts electrical energy—or chemical energy from a gas stove—to heat energy to cook our food.

Consider This

Inventors have built dance floors that convert mechanical energy produced by dancing feet into electrical energy to power lights and more! Can you think of other ways that mechanical energy can be converted to another form of energy?

Mechanical Energy Through History

Humans have always used mechanical energy to get work done, even when they didn't have a name for it. Waterpower was used to grind grain during the Middle Ages. Later, people used the mechanical energy of wind to do work. Windmills were used to grind grain into flour and to pump water. Today modern windmills, called wind **turbines**, produce electricity for many communities.

Water mills use the mechanical energy of moving water to turn wheels and power mechanical processes such as grinding grain.

One of the most important inventions to come out of steam power was the steam train. This allowed people to travel great distances faster than ever before.

The Industrial Revolution was a period of major changes in the way products were made. More than 200 years ago people began to invent machines to do the work that individuals did by hand before that time. People also built factories where those machines could be used to make many products at once. Inventors created power sources to run the machines. For example, steam engines used the power of steam to produce mechanical energy. They were used for many years to power trains, cars, ships, and other machines. Today, fossil fuels provide mechanical energy to the same machines.

WORD WISE

TURBINES ARE ENGINES THAT DEPEND ON MOVING WATER, STEAM, OR AIR TO SPIN A SERIES OF BLADES.

Sustainable Energy

Many sources of energy used to power machines are renewable, which means that they are not likely to run out. Examples include the sun, wind, and water. Water and wind were used to operate mills for hundreds of years because there was a constant supply of both.

Wind turbines and solar panels can harness renewable energy from the wind and sun to provide electricity to cities.

Hydroelectric dams use the energy from moving water to create electricity.

Today, machines are more complicated. They rely on other sources of power, such as electricity. However, the renewable energy sources are still useful. When the blades of a wind turbine spin, they convert the mechanical energy of the wind into electrical energy. Wind turbines can work alone or in a group, called a wind farm. In a similar way, other machines in rivers and oceans can use the mechanical energy of moving water to produce electrical energy. That electrical energy can then be used to power large machines. These large machines then, in turn, use mechanical energy to get work done.

Consider This

Certain places have better renewable energy sources than others. What renewable energy sources exist where you live?

Fossil Fuels

Modern machines don't just do work on their own, they need another form of energy to make them run. Wind and waterpower are used to create some of that energy. However, about 80 percent of the world's energy comes from burning fossil fuels. Fossil fuels include petroleum (oil), coal, and natural gas. The burning of these fossil fuels produces heat. The heat energy is often converted into mechanical or electrical energy.

One of the earliest forms of fossil fuels humans first used—and still use today—is coal.

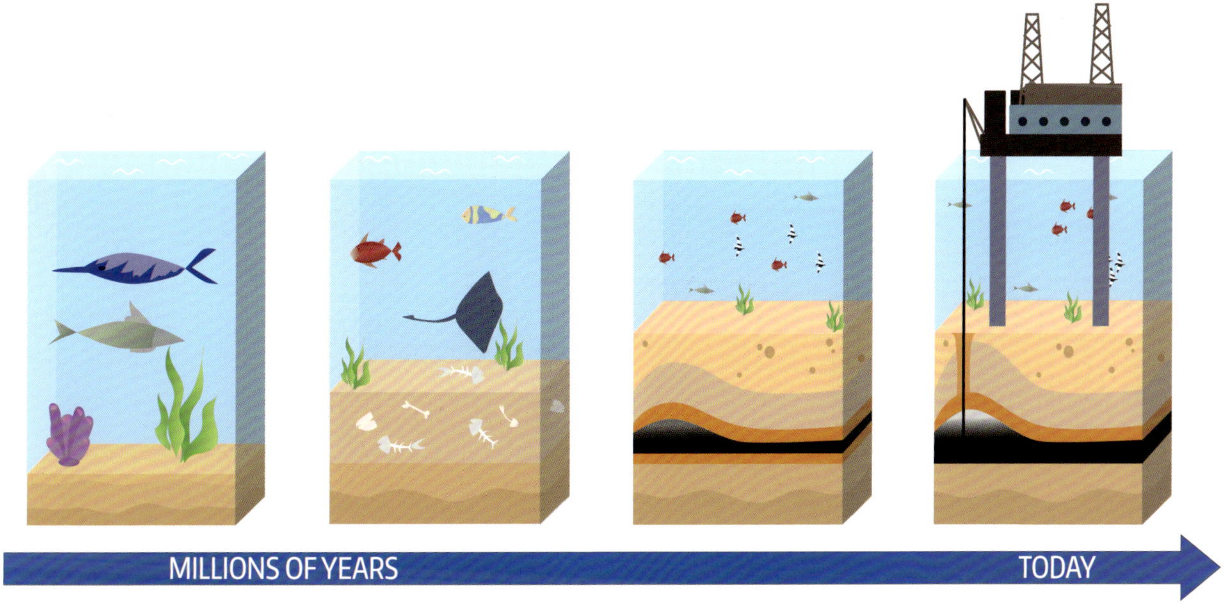

Today, oil companies often build ocean rigs to dig for the fossil fuels under the sea floor. This oil formed over millions of years from the remains of dead sea life.

Fossil fuels, like fossils, are the remains of plants and animals that lived long ago. These resources can take thousands or millions of years to form. The planet's supply of fossil fuels is limited. Fossil fuels are called nonrenewable resources. Once they are used up, they will be gone forever. Many countries are pushing people to rely more on renewable energy sources.

Consider This

Why can't we replace fossil fuels once they are used? How long does it take for them to form?

Problems with Fossil Fuels

Fossil fuels have been the primary source of energy for humans for hundreds of years. However, fossil fuels are nonrenewable. They also harm the environment. When petroleum and coal burn, they release harmful gases. These cause pollution, which can make people sick or make it hard for people to breathe. Scientists think that burning fossil fuels also adds extra gases to the air that trap heat in the atmosphere. They think that this has led to a problem called global warming.

Many people want to use renewable energy sources instead of fossil fuels. Renewable energy sources such as wind, water, and solar power will not run out. However, switching to these energy sources is expensive. People would have to make major changes to the systems that are already in place. In addition, some technologies for renewable energy are still relatively new. They need further research and development. But they're becoming more and more available in some parts of the world.

Cars that use fossil fuels for power let out emissions that cloud the air and harm people's health.

compare and contrast

What are some advantages and disadvantages to using alternative energy sources and fossil fuels?

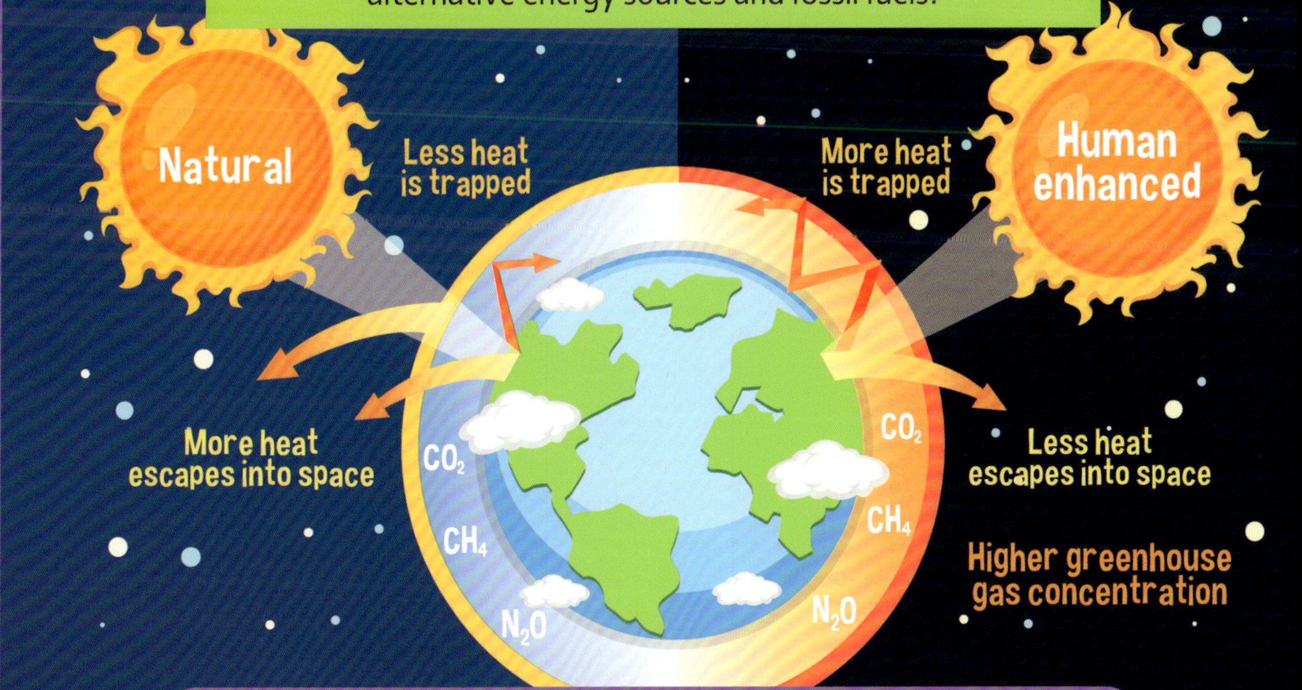

Extra gases such as carbon dioxide (CO_2), methane (CH_4), and nitrous oxide (N_2O) in the atmosphere can cause more heat to be trapped in Earth's atmosphere. This is called the greenhouse effect.

Changing Energy Use

Many people try to protect nature from the harms caused by fossil fuel use. This is called conservation. People who care about conservation try to preserve natural resources so they will still be around in the future. They also try to keep the environment clean and healthy.

Activists often demonstrate to encourage governments and companies to reduce their reliance on fossil fuels.

People who live close to work or school can choose to walk there. Good public transportation—often only in big cities—also helps reduce emissions.

Conservation can be hard because it can require people to give up some conveniences. For example, cars that run on gasoline are everywhere. They make traveling easy, but they also produce a lot of air pollution. To have cleaner air, people can choose to drive less and walk more. Understanding where our energy comes from is a responsibility we have. Those who are able can choose to use the mechanical energy from our legs to walk rather than to use nonrenewable energy sources by riding in cars.

Consider This

Conserving nonrenewable energy sources can involve healthful, fun exercise! What sports activities that involve the use of mechanical energy by your body do you most enjoy doing?

Glossary

alternative Offering or expressing a choice.

atmosphere The layer of gases that surrounds Earth.

battery A container that stores chemical energy and converts it to electric energy when used.

convert To change from one thing into another.

electron An elementary particle that has a negative charge of electricity and travels around the nucleus, or center, of an atom.

environment The physical surroundings on Earth, such as air, oceans, and trees.

friction When two things rub against one another.

Industrial Revolution A period in history beginning in the 1700s when people began to use machines to make products.

lever A bar used to pry or move something.

Middle Ages A period in European history that came between ancient and modern times and lasted from about 500 to 1500 CE.

natural resources Something found in nature that can be used by people, such as sunlight, water, or plants.

pulley A small wheel with a rope or chain around its edge, used to change the direction of the force applied for lifting.

wedge A piece of wood or metal with a pointed edge used especially to split wood or rocks and to lift heavy weights.

For More Information

Books

Bunting, Philip. *Super Power: Renewable Energy: What It Is, How We Get It, and Why We Need It.* Richmond, Australia: Bright Light, 2024.

Martin, Claudia. *Ecstatic (and Excellent) Energy: Enter a World of Petrifying Power!* Buffalo, NY: Gareth Stevens Publishing, 2025.

Websites

Kids Britannica: Mechanical Energy
www.kids.britannica.com/kids/article/mechanical-energy/628738
Read more and watch videos about mechanical energy on how it helps us do work.

Energy Kids: Forms of Energy
www.eia.gov/kids/what-is-energy/forms-of-energy.php
Learn all about the different forms of energy.

Index

A
animals, 4, 9

B
batteries, 12, 13

C
chemical energy, 4, 9, 12, 13, 16, 18, 19

E
electrical energy, 5, 6, 7, 12, 19, 20, 22, 23, 24
electrolyte, 13
electrons, 5, 7, 13

F
food, 4, 6, 7, 9, 13, 18, 19
fossil fuel, 24, 25, 26, 27, 28, 29
friction, 13, 14

H
heat energy, 5, 12, 13, 14, 19, 24
human body, 4, 5, 7, 9, 12, 15, 17, 18

I
Industrial Revolution, 21

K
kinetic energy, 6, 7, 8, 9, 14, 17

L
light energy, 5, 12

M
machines, 5, 9, 16, 21, 22, 23, 24
mass, 10, 11, 15, 16

P
plants, 4
potential energy, 6, 7, 8, 9, 10, 14, 16, 17

S
sound energy, 5
sustainable energy, 22, 23, 25, 26, 28, 29